@IG_ROHIT

FOREWORD

WHY YOU SHOULD READ THIS BOOK ?

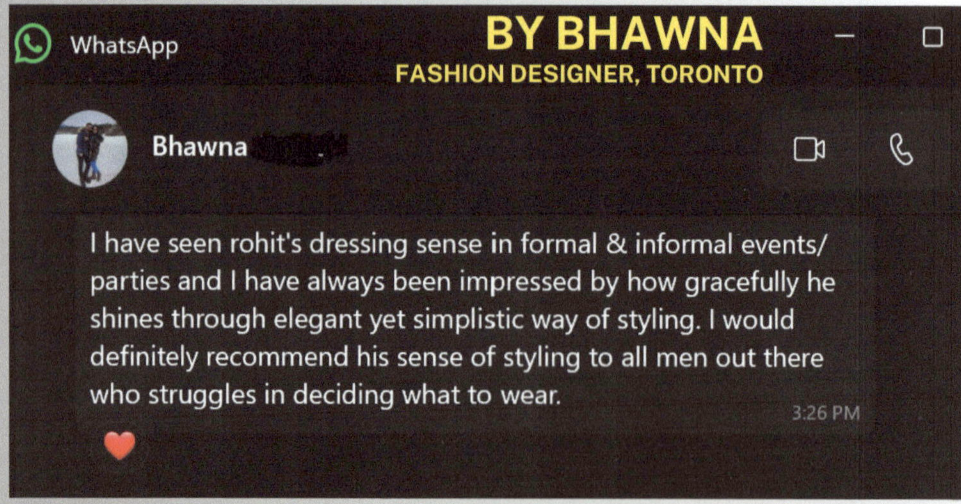

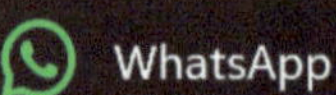

@IG_ROHIT

TESTIMONIALS

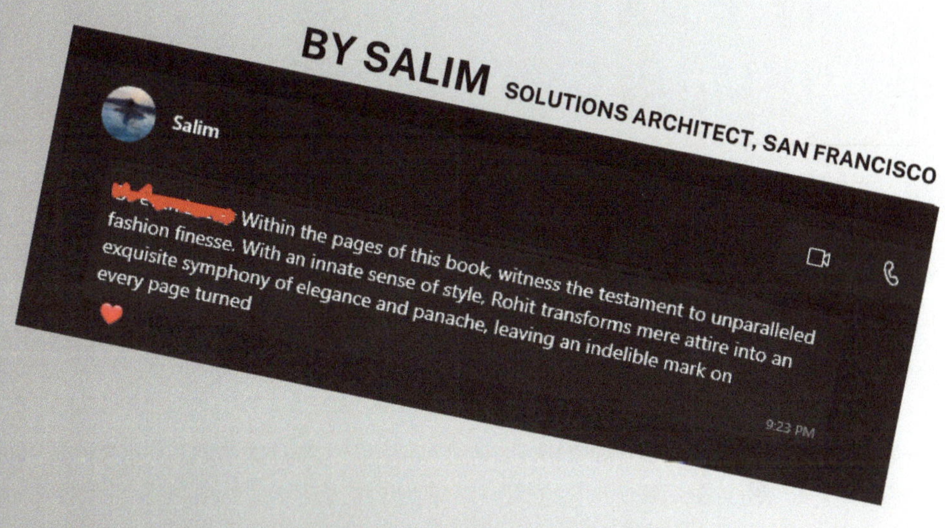

@IG_ROHIT

PREFACE
WHY THIS BOOK CAME INTO BEING ?

Just so others don't have to spend a decade like me, to learn these principles, I am giving away what I learnt, for FREE.

I always thought dressing well meant buying expensive clothes. And, I never had enough money or the justification when I had the money - as to why looking good is only achieved with expensive clothes.

My dad always said "Dress simple" and
Don Draper said - "Make it simple, but significant".

So, about a decade ago, I decided to educate myself on fashion, and started digging deep into the rabbit hole of what makes a person look good ? How does fashion work ? What is this thing we call style ?

And, over time I tried and failed 100s of times to learn about style and fashion.

@IG_ROHIT

INTRODUCTION

I tried to distill knowledge from my decade long research into a handful of pages with bullet points that you can immediately absorb and apply, starting today.

Feel free to modify as per your taste and remember, these are mere guidelines. So feel free to use and throw whatever you like.

But, these are the principles that work for me every day successfully, so I hope it helps you too.

WHAT ARE THE BROAD STROKES THAT MATTER ?

TIP #1

PICK YOUR MASCULINE ARCHETYPE

ROCKER GUY

Everybody can identify what they relate to, internally. What is your vibe ? What relates to you the most ?

@IG_ROHIT

CHILL RELAXED GUY

Are you the <u>guy in Suits</u> ? A <u>chill relaxed vibe guy</u> with long hair and loose linen clothes ? A <u>leather jacket wearing biker type</u> with boots and top 3 buttons of their shirt open ? A <u>rocker</u> punk type with lots of necklaces, piercing and all blacks ? A <u>rapper hip hop guy</u> with heavy bracelets and jewelry ? A sports jockey type with baseball cap and polo t-shirts ?

SUITS GUY

Find your archetype and write it down. You can have multiple things that you relate to around different times of your life. But, one of them will be stronger than others. What is that one type ?

@IG_ROHIT

BIKER GUY

Type on google that archetype and study what kind of clothes they wear ?

For instance, the guy in suits won't typically be wearing baseball cap. Unless you're combining 2 styles but that is recommended only when you have mastered the basics.

RAPPER HIP HOP GUY

Once you master one or two styles - then the world is your oyster, and you can combine any style with anything as per your liking.

But if you're starting new, I recommend stick to the basic archetype and master it fully.

@IG_ROHIT

PROCESS TO FOLLOW

Once you know what your goal is, now you can start preparing your wardrobe over time to have more items from that archetype, and give away the clothing that doesn't go along with it.

Choose 2 outfits from google images, and make a resembling outfit like them from your wardrobe. Make sure you match everything around it. Starting from the colors and the fabric, to the shoes and accessories.

Wear those outfits out with your friends, and be on the lookout if people are liking it or not. If it's well received, save it as one of your combination outfits. If its not getting compliments, then it still needs refinement.

TIP #2

UNDERSTAND YOUR COLORS

HOW MUCH CONTRAST ?

The types of contrast you choose in your colors, depend on the contrast you have between your hair color and skin color.

The purpose of fashion is to elevate your face and bring attention to it.

If there isn't enough contrast between your hair and skin, then a bright contrast in your clothing will make your face look pale compared to your clothes.

And, you never want your face to look pale.

FINALIZE YOUR BASE AND NON-BASE COLORS

When making outfits, you want to have a base color. This is your canvas where your painting will be drawn. White, and Black are called base colors. Sometimes brown is considered base too, but personally I'm not a big fan of brown.

Usually, I put base color as my shirt or t-shirt and wear my blazer or another layer on top.

Upon your base color is where you put a splash (remember, just a splash) of some bright color.
Eg. red scarf on white tshirt, or blue tie on black shirt for an evening party.

Advanced level splashing can also be done with pocket scarfs but only after mastering the basics.

HOW MANY COLORS SHOULD YOU INCLUDE ?

In any outfit, try to limit the number of colors to TWO. And yes, 2 shades of green don't count as one, but two colors in that outfit.

Advanced level (after mastering the basics) can sometimes pull off 3 colors in the palette but I'd highly recommend beginners to stick to 2 colors per outfit.

And, black or white being base colors (eg. white t-shirt with black jeans) still count as one color when worn together. So, adding third color onto is to be considered one base color and one non-base color.

Never combine more than 1 splash color with White or Blacks. Those only look good on runway fashion. Blue pants with Red shirt and Yellow scarf looks good on google images, but not in real life.

TIP #3

ALWAYS MATCH YOUR LEATHERS

LEATHERS GIVE MASCULINE LOOK

Leather Belt and Leather Shoes should match in color. Browns with browns, and blacks with blacks. This gives you a well thought masculine look.

@IG_ROHIT

Eg. the matching leather jacket with his belt's color gives it a more thoughtful aesthetic look

Different shades of brown mean different colors, so try to get them as close to each other as possible. Based on your archetype you can decide what style of leather shoes you want.

The guy wearing suits won't typically match his suit with long leather boots, and the biker guy will look off-fashion in dress shoes.

@IG_ROHIT

COMMIT TO IT

Remember, whenever in confusion, go back to your archetype and THINK -

---

What would my archetype wear in this situation ?

During summers, its hard to wear leathers, so if you're wearing sports lightweight shoes, try to match them with sporty belts instead of leather belts.

Remember, if you're targeting a sporty casual look, don't half ass it. Look committed to it. That's what makes it fashionable.

TIP #4

MATCH YOUR METALS

EXAMPLES

Either have all gold or all silver. Gold chain on the neck with silver watch and black bracelet looks mismatched and it's not aesthetic.

AVOID TOO MANY COLORS

Remember the goal of fashion is to look pleasing to the eye.

The less number of colors your eye has to track, the easier it is for the eyes to relax and soak the beauty. Too many colors overwhelm the eyes.

Symmetry is the foundation of beauty

Always keep your archetype in mind. If your archetype is casual baseball hat sporty guy, will he wear *long chains* like hip hop rappers do ? No, it would look out of place.

Stick to fundamentals and master them before mixing 2 archetypes at the advanced level.

When you have figured out what jewelries go well with your archetype, you can refine that to the specifics. Eg. what style of watch to wear, what style of chain, what style of bracelet ? Each accessory has different styles in it, so make sure to choose the style that goes well with your aesthetics and archetype.

@IG_ROHIT

TIP #5

WEAR CLEAN SHOES

Your shoes make a statement that we often ignore. When someone sees your shoes are top notch, they know you have put in thought to the rest of your clothes.

@IG_ROHIT

GET SHOES MATCHING YOUR ARCHETYPE

Boat shoes go well with casual summery look, while sturdy leather boots go well with biker look. Dress shoes don't go well without a blazer and/or a shirt unless you do it armed with specific knowledge of what you're doing.
Remember to keep their comfort in mind not to hurt your feet walking all day.

@IG_ROHIT

BONUS TIP

STAY GROOMED

EXAMPLES

Stay groomed. Remember, the goal of fashion is to bring attention to your face. But, that won't be of much help if your face looks unkempt.

Get regular haircuts. And, know your style. Don't put yourself at the mercy of your hair dresser.

@IG_ROHIT

PROCESS TO FOLLOW

Stand in front of your mirror and draw an outline with a soap of your face (excluding the hair).

From this process, you'll know the shape of your face - whether it is oval, or square, or triangle.

Once you know the shape of your face, you can make adjustments to it. Remember the hair and beard are there to accentuate your natural shape.

This natural shape from the above exercise is your starting point, and your end goal is to accessorize your face (with hairstyle and beard) that makes it look masculine (or feminine).

If you have a round chin, do things that make the bottom of your face have edges (simulating strong jawline). If you have a pointy chin, you can extend the base by having a beard that adds some width to your chin. The masculine traits are strong jawline and big wide forehead. And, these can be imitated with adding layers on top (hairstyle) and bottom (with beard)

If not full haircut, always make sure your sides and back are trimmed.

Sharp sideburns make you look groomed even if top hair is long which at that point, starts looking intentional as a style.

@IG_ROHIT

CONCLUSION

All this is not the entirety. There is so much more that goes into it. But, hopefully this gives you the broad strokes to start your journey.

At any point, feel free to reach out to me -

 www.instagram.com/ig_rohit

 https://www.facebook.com/timelinerohit

 everydaystylebyrohit@gmail.com

We have a monthly newsletter where we send out FREE tips for upgrading your fashion.

Be sure to subscribe to that.

In the meantime, if you found this helpful - I am working on a video course that will have much more than just 5 tips above. Keep an eye out for it.

@IG_ROHIT

CONCLUSION

Since you've read until here, you have passed the test - where I will be helping out first 50 clients for free with their fashion, to find their personal style.

Reach out to me with subject/title as
"FINISHED EBOOK"
and I will help you.

@IG_ROHIT

THANK YOU

www.ingramcontent.com/pod-product-compliance
Lightning Source LLC
Chambersburg PA
CBHW040247240726
48664CB00001B/302